# UNDERSTANDING
# RELIGIONS

# Food and
# Fasting

## Deirdre Burke

**Wayland**

# Understanding Religions

**Birth Customs**
**Death Customs**
**Food and Fasting**
**Initiation Customs**
**Marriage Customs**
**Pilgrimages and Journeys**

---

**About this book**

This book looks at issues concerning food and its place in the lives of believers from six major religious traditions. Food is used in many customs, including weekly services and special festivals.

Food laws spring from fundamental beliefs in many religions and **Food and Fasting** provides an introduction to these beliefs. Each chapter deals with one aspect of eating or fasting, so that readers may compare different attitudes and beliefs closely. The importance of fasting in some religions, and the many symbolic uses of food are included to show the different ways in which people remember their God through eating or not eating.

The quotations in the book will encourage children to look at the religious practices of their own communities and those of their friends. Teachers will find that elements of each chapter can be used as starting points for project work.

---

Editor: Joanna Housley
Designer: Malcolm Walker

This edition published in 1995 by
Wayland (Publishers) Limited

First published in 1992 by
Wayland (Publishers) Limited
61 Western Road, Hove
East Sussex, BN3 1JD, England

**British Library Cataloguing in Publication Data**
Burke, Deirdre
    Food and Fasting. (Understanding Religions Series)
    I. Title  II. Series
    291.4

**HARDBACK** ISBN 0-7502-0421-4

**PAPERBACK** ISBN 0-7502-1667-0

Typeset by Kudos Editorial and Design Services
Printed in Italy by G Canale C.S.p.A. Turin

# Contents

Words that appear in **bold** in the text are
explained in the glossary on page 30.

# Introduction

Please sit down and join us for some food. We are about to eat our school lunch. What would you like to eat for your lunch?

'Cheeseburger and chips for me, please.' said Kelly, a Roman Catholic.

'I don't want a cheeseburger,' said Harpreet, a Sikh, 'as it is made from beef and I don't eat cows, so I'll have a vegetable samosa.'

'Me next!' said Samina, a Muslim girl. 'I am going to have the **halal** chicken as I don't eat pork or meat that is not halal.'

'I'll have a vegetable samosa too.' said Jason, a Hindu. 'I don't want the cheeseburger as the cow is a holy animal.'

'I can't eat the cheeseburger,' said Daniel, a Jewish boy, 'because the meat is not **kosher**, and I don't eat meat and cheese together.'

Do you and your friends have talks like this at your meal times? If you do, you may already know that Sikhs and Hindus do not eat beef and that Muslims and Jews will not eat pork. Are there any foods that your religion tells you not to eat?

Have you ever thought about why you eat some foods and not others? Do you know why some people never eat

*Above* Children at this school are able to choose meals that are halal or **vegetarian**.

certain foods, or why special foods are eaten at important times of the year? Perhaps the strangest question of all is 'Why do some people go without food by fasting?'

The answers to some of these questions should become clear as we investigate some of the customs that religious people have about food.

# What we eat

Would you like something to eat? How many times have you been asked this question? Probably hundreds of times. If you are hungry you might just say 'Yes please', knowing that your parents will give you good food. Some people do not eat certain foods that are bad for their health. Such people may be rare, but throughout the world you will find people who eat some foods and not others because of their religion.

## Food laws and beliefs

Many religions have food laws that state what people can eat and how food should be prepared. Some of these laws come from the belief that certain foods are unclean, and others come from the belief that certain foods are holy.

Buddhists do not have specific laws concerning food, but general laws called Precepts are followed. The first of these Precepts is not to kill or harm any living creature. This means that it is a sin to kill animals and many Buddhists are vegetarians. They do not eat meat.

## Beliefs about food

The Hindu tradition teaches that certain animals are holy and special and for that reason they should not be killed and eaten. Jason told us that he cannot eat beef because it is the meat of a cow, which is a holy animal to Hindus. In one Hindu holy book it is written 'all who eat the flesh or permit the **slaughter** of cows will rot in hell for as many years as there are hairs on the body of the cow'.

Like Buddhists, Hindus also respect all creatures. They believe that all living

*Below* Buddhist monks eat only one meal a day. They only eat enough food to keep their bodies healthy, and do not eat after midday so that they can meditate without feeling drowsy.

things have a soul which will be reborn in another body. Hindus have influenced Sikh eating habits. Sikhs do not eat beef, even though the teachings of their **Gurus** do not forbid it.

Christians do not have any particular food laws. The way Christians think of food has been shaped by a vision (a special dream) that St. Peter had. In this vision Peter was shown animals and told to eat. At first he hesitated because he had been brought up a Jew and thought that some animals were unclean. He was shown in the vision that it is not what you eat that makes you unclean but your own thoughts and actions.

Some religions say that certain animals are unclean and should not be eaten. This is why Muslims and Jews do not eat pork. Samina says 'You should not eat

*Left* To Muslims and Jews, the pig is an unclean animal.

Jason, a Hindu, aged 7: 'We can't eat cows because they are holy, they were created at the beginning of time. Also, I like to drink milk, so I don't want to eat cows if they give me milk.'

food with animal fat in it, or pig. We cannot even touch pigs.'

Food that Muslims eat is called halal, which means food that is permitted. Food that is not permitted is called **haram**. Halal food will not have any pig products in it. This covers foods like bread, cakes and sweets that could have animal fat in them. It is also important that the animal is killed and prepared in the correct way.

The Jewish religion has rules that cover every mouthful of food taken. In the Torah (the Jewish holy book) there are laws that state which animals, fish, birds and insects are clean. Animals are clean if they chew the cud (this means they have more than one stomach for digesting plants), and have a cloven (divided) hoof. Sheep and goats are clean, while the pig, camel and hippopotamus are unclean. Some Jews explain that the laws forbid all animals with evil instincts, animals that eat each other or who have dirty habits like eating rubbish. The belief behind this is that you may develop the qualities that the animal has if you eat its flesh.

Some religions also have rules on how food should be prepared. These laws may cover how to kill the animal. Samina says, 'When we kill a chicken we say a prayer to thank Allah (God) for the food, so that it will be fresh and not poisonous.'

## Killed in the name of God

Jews, Muslims and Sikhs all have their own way of killing animals. In each case the animal is killed by one single cut with a knife and a special prayer is said. The Sikh prayer is 'Truth is immortal' and this way of killing is known as *Jhatka*.

For Muslims halal food must be killed and prepared in the correct way. Without the right prayer a chicken will be haram. Once the animal has been killed all the blood must be drained from the body. Halal meat is sold at shops which display the sign 'Halal'.

Most Jews only eat meat that is kosher. This means that the meat is from a clean animal that has been killed in the correct way, and drained of blood. This method of slaughter is known as *Shechitah*.

Many people think that ritual slaughter is cruel as the animals are not stunned before they are killed. Jews and Muslims kill in this way because they are following their religion. The prayer shows that they can only kill God's creatures in the way that they believe God told them to. They show that they are not taking the killing of one of God's creatures lightly.

## Special preparation of food

The Hindu religion has rules which say who may prepare food for others. Some Hindus still follow rules which divide

*Above* In a halal butcher's stall the meat has been prepared according to Muslim rules.

*Above* This Hindu family in India make sure that the ground and the banana leaves are clean before they eat.

people into **castes** and prevent those of different castes eating with each other. Hindus take great care to keep food away from dirt. Care is also taken to make sure that leftover food is thrown away, to prevent the spread of germs.

Many religious people will say a prayer whilst preparing food. Harpreet's mother says the words, 'God is one' when she is preparing the food. She will also cover her head before cooking or serving food. Other Sikhs may take a bath before cooking to make sure that they are clean. Traditions also say that

11

there should be no gossip when the food is prepared in the **gurdwara**.

The Jewish food laws put all food that is allowed into three types: meat, dairy products (like milk and butter) and parve (like fruit and vegetables). Meat needs to be carefully prepared by using salt to wash out all the blood. Meat and milk must never be cooked or eaten together. Jews cannot eat buttered potatoes with roast chicken. Nor can they have a pudding afterwards which has cream or custard or ice-cream. Many Jewish homes have two sinks, two worktops, two cookers and at least two sets of pots and pans, cutlery and crockery. An extra set is needed for the festival of Passover, when no yeast (or raising agent) should be used.

## Food laws have reasons

There are many reasons why these laws are important. Some religions believe that certain foods are unclean and should not be eaten. Religions which only allow the killing of animals in a certain way may be trying to make sure that believers always remember God. Those religions, like Islam and Judaism, which do not allow followers to eat blood, may be trying to create a horror of bloodshed. Some religions use food laws to prevent followers from eating with people who do not belong to the same religion.

*Above* Sikh women cover their heads and say prayers before they prepare the food in the gurdwara.

# How to eat

What do you do before you eat? Have you seen other people doing something special before they eat?

## Words and actions before eating

Many people wash their hands and say special words before and after eating. Almost everyone washes their hands before eating, to prevent any germs from entering the body. For people who belong to a religion it may be important to say special words even when they carry out ordinary, everyday activities.

Jews often say special **blessings** when eating particular foods – the number of blessings will depend on what they are eating. Saying blessings is their way of remembering God and thinking of the things that God has done for them. Blessings are also a way of saying that things are holy and belong to God. **Orthodox Jews** tend to follow their traditions closely. There is a long prayer for meals eaten by three or more men and a shorter one for less than three. Part of the shorter prayer shows how Jews are grateful to God: 'Blessed are you, O Lord our God, King of the Universe, who feeds the whole world with goodness.' The blessing also reminds

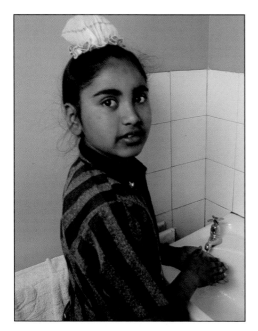

*Below* Harpreet, a Sikh boy, washes his hands before eating.

James, a Christian, aged 9, describes grace: 'Saying grace is a good idea as it blesses the food, which means that the food has been made special by Jesus. After eating we say 'Thank you God for this wonderful food'.'

the people of what God has done for them in the past and how they are saying the same words as their **ancestors** said in the past.

Christians can choose to say **grace** before a meal. It is a way of thanking God for the gift of food, and making eating special. This grace is over a hundred years old: 'Bless us, O Lord, and these thy gifts, which we are about to receive of thy bounty, through Christ our Lord. Amen.' These special words help Christians to remember their belief that God created them and provides them with all they need.

Hindus and Sikhs do not have to say any set prayers before meals, but many do. Some of these prayers may be short, like the prayer Sikhs say in the gurdwara before eating. They cover their heads, as a sign of respect, then hold a chappati in their hands and say special words. For special occasions at the gurdwara a

*Right* This Hindu family sprinkles water around the food before eating.

*Below* These Indian ladies make sure that they only use the right hand for eating. The right hand is only used for clean activities.

longer prayer may be said: 'God is the provider for everyone, there is no shortage.' At home a short prayer, 'God is one', may be said.

A custom that many Hindus follow at home is to sprinkle water over the food and ask God to bless it. A small amount of all the food to be eaten may be taken from the table and given to animals or birds. After eating most people want to give thanks for the food, just as you probably say thank you to people who give you things. For Muslims, Hindus and Sikhs it is important to wash their hands after eating. This custom probably comes from the use of fingers for eating.

The next time you sit down to eat a meal you might think about the things that some religious people do to make eating special.

# Food at places of worship

## Offering and sharing food

What do people eat in places of worship? Sharing food is important to people. Some religions have food constantly on offer in their place of worship, others use food either during or after the main service.

In Hindu temples the priest will offer the food, usually water, milk, sweets

*Below*   After the food has been offered during the Hindu 'fire service', it will be given to worshippers along with fruit, nuts and sweets that have been blessed.

and fruit, during the service, which may take place twice daily. The food is placed on a tray with **purified** water, **incense** and a lamp. The food is offered to the gods and then shared out to the worshippers. It becomes *prashad* (holy food) when it is shared. Water and milk are placed in the worshipper's right hand with a spoon. Many Hindu temples have a special weekly service. This 'fire service' is called '*Havan*' and it may be followed by a **communal** vegetarian meal.

## Communal meals – eating together

The idea of a communal meal is very important in Sikhism. Food is given by worshippers to be cooked by volunteers

*Below* The *kirpan* is one of the five signs that a Sikh wears. Here it is used to stir the ingredients of the *karah parshad*.

Uma, A Sikh girl, aged 8, is being served with the food that everyone eats together in the gurdwara:
'After the service at the gurdwara, everyone can share a meal in the kitchen, called the *guru ka langa*. It means the guru's kitchen. Lots of people help make the food, then anyone can join in when we eat it.'

in the communal kitchen, called the *guru ka langa*. This means the guru's kitchen. Many Sikhs help out by preparing, cooking and serving the food. Hymns are sung and prayers are chanted while the food is being prepared. A small portion of each food that is cooked is blessed by offering it to God. This food is then mixed in with the rest of the food, which blesses the whole meal.

The Sikh teacher Guru Nanak began the custom of eating together in the gurdwara to show that everyone is equal. The food supplied shows that God provides for all the needs of the people, in worship and in eating food. The communal idea is also shown in the sharing of *karah parshad*, which is a mixture of flour, butter, sugar and water. This is prepared in a ritual way. A prayer is said and a special sword called the

*kirpan* is used to mix the ingredients together. This **symbolizes** the strength that the community get from worshipping and eating together, as members of one family.

## Symbolic eating

At the heart of Christian worship is the **Eucharist**, which is also called Holy Communion, the Lord's Supper or the Mass. At this time Christians remember the Last Supper Jesus shared with his disciples (followers). At this supper Jesus broke bread and poured wine in a simple ceremony which he told his followers to do in memory of him. Many Christians take Holy Communion as a symbol of the death and **resurrection** of Jesus, so that the gifts of the bread and the wine 'may be to us his body and his blood'.

Many Christians believe that the bread and the wine actually change into the body and blood of Jesus. This is why some Catholics fast before taking communion as they do not want the holy food to come into contact with any ordinary food that is in their stomachs.

The breaking and sharing of bread is also important in Judaism. On *Shabbat* (the weekly day of rest) the Jewish community will make *Kiddush*, a ceremony in which bread and wine are blessed. The bread is usually a plaited loaf called *challah*. Two loaves are used to remember the two portions of manna,

*Above*   This Christian minister places the communion bread in worshippers' mouths. In some churches the bread is put into the hands of the worshipper.

*Right*  A special *challah* is used at a Jewish wedding. The bread has salt sprinkled on it before it is eaten.

which was the special food that the Israelites were given when they were in the **wilderness**. *Kiddush*, which means making holy, takes place in homes for the three meals of *Shabbat*. In the synagogue the congregation will make a *Kiddush* together on Friday evening and Saturday morning.

Daniel, a Jew, aged 10: 'Every Friday night we have the *Shabbat* (or Sabbath) meal. The grown-ups bless and drink a glass of wine. Under the cloth on this table is a special bread called *challah*. It is plaited, and there are two loaves which are blessed and eaten.'

# Food and festivals

Festivals are fun times remembering important people or events. At such special times people may celebrate by eating special foods. Do you celebrate a festival where you eat special food? Some festivals have their own flavour and when people think of the festival they often think of the foods that are eaten. Can you think of any foods that are eaten at festivals?

## Hidden messages in food

Do you know why mince pies are eaten at Christmas, the time when Christians celebrate the birth of Jesus Christ? When he was born, Jesus' crib was a **manger**, and hundreds of years ago mince pies used to be called 'crib pies'. They were made in the shape of a manger or a cradle, with a pastry baby on top.

## Crosses and eggs

Easter is another Christian festival that has special foods. Hot cross buns are traditionally eaten on Good Friday, the day on which Jesus died. He was killed by being nailed to a cross and left to die. The cross on the buns reminds Christians of how Jesus died. The spices in the buns remind them of the spices that were

*Below* Kelly, a Christian, shows her friends a crib pie – a mince pie with a pastry baby on top.

*Above* The foods eaten at the Seder meal all have special meanings. They remind Jews of the Israelites' escape from slavery.

used to prepare Jesus' body for the tomb.

Some Christians eat chocolate Easter eggs. Eggs are a symbol of new life and of the Resurrection of Jesus. Christians believe that Jesus came back to life three days after he died: this is called the Resurrection. They eat Easter eggs as a celebration of his new life.

## Remembering events through food

Jews also have special foods that are eaten only at certain festivals. At Passover a special meal called the Seder meal is eaten. Children ask why they only eat *matzah* (unleavened bread which has no yeast in it) when at other times they can eat bread with yeast. The answer to this question takes them back over three thousand years to the time of the **Exodus** from Egypt. At this time the people of Israel worked as slaves in Egypt. The Seder meal relives their experiences.

Food is dipped in salt to remember the tears they cried as slaves. Bitter herbs recall the bitterness of slavery. Unleavened bread or *matzah* is eaten to symbolize the fact that the Israelites could not wait for the bread to rise when they hurried away from Egypt. Fresh greens are a symbol of spring and new life and they remind people that the Jews were given the chance to start a new life in obedience to God's commands.

Other Jewish festivals have special foods that are associated with the theme of the festival. At *Hanukkah*, the 'miracle of the oil' is celebrated, when enough oil for one day lasted for eight days. In memory of this miracle foods are eaten that have been cooked in oil, like *latkes* (potato pancakes) or doughnuts.

## Sweet foods

Another Jewish festival, *Rosh Hashanah*, uses food in a similar way to other religions. This is the New Year festival and it is a custom to eat honey in the hope that the new year will be a sweet one. Hindus also eat sweet foods at festival times. The sweet taste of the food is symbolic of the sweetness of the time that a festival, such as **Diwali**, recalls. The birthdays of many of the

*Above* At *Rosh Hashanah* Jews often dip apple in honey and say, 'May it be your will, Lord our God and God of our fathers, to renew unto us a good and pleasant year'.

*Left* The Hindu Diwali festival is celebrated at the family shrine with lighted candles and sweet foods.

gods are remembered by eating sweet things. The God Krishna liked molasses as a child, so many worshippers will eat pancakes with molasses on his birthday, which are made from yoghurt and honey. The special *prashad* offered to the God Rama on his birthday may also be made from molasses.

Eating sweet things at happy times also applies to many Muslim festivals. The birthday of the Prophet Muhammad is celebrated by a special gathering where Muslims eat traditional sweets. A Muslim prayer expresses thanks for good food that is eaten at Id-ul-Fitr: 'O Lord, send down to us food from heaven so that it becomes a day of rejoicing.' Id-ul-Fitr is the celebration at the end of Ramadan (the month of fasting). It lasts for three days. During Id-ul-Fitr Muslims visit relatives and friends and eat the special foods that have been prepared.

*Right* A Muslim family in China celebrates the end of Ramadan by eating special biscuits.

# When not to eat

Some people prepare themselves for a festival by fasting. The word 'fast' means that a person is not eating. This may be for a certain length of time, or for certain parts of the day, or it may mean that certain foods are not eaten. Some fasts are compulsory for all believers, and others people can choose to do.

Have you ever done without something for a special purpose? Maybe you have saved your pocket money to buy something for yourself or for someone special. Religious people make a similar kind of **sacrifice** when they give up eating for a time. They feel that going without food, at particular times, can be a form of worship.

*Left* Samina shows her class how she will break her fast with a glass of water and a date.

## A time to fast

Muslims fast during the month of Ramadan. They do not eat or drink anything during the hours of daylight (from sunrise to sunset). This is a compulsory fast which everyone should do if they are old enough and fit enough. Young children learn how to fast by going without sweets or snacks between meals and gradually build up to going without one meal a day. It can be very hard for Muslims living in hot countries to go without water during the day. The fast is broken at sunset each day, when most Muslims will follow the example of the prophet Muhammad and eat a date with some water. This is followed by a proper meal and it is recommended that all Muslims should eat a nourishing meal early in the morning before sunrise.

*Right* Before the *iftar* meal, which breaks the fast every evening during Ramadan, a special prayer is said: 'God, I have fasted for you, and I have believed in you and with your food I break the fast.'

This fast, which is called *Sawm*, is one of the **five pillars of Islam**. Fasting helps Muslims realize their dependence on God, and show that they are prepared for any sufferings that may follow from obeying God. Fasting helps to bring the community together, as all Muslims, whether rich or poor, share in the same experience. It also helps those who normally eat well to remember what it feels like to be hungry, so they will think to help those in need.

Yom Kippur is a required fast for Jews. It lasts for one whole day, from sunset to sunset. This is the day when Jews feel they are closest to God. They start preparing for Yom Kippur ten days earlier, at *Rosh Hashanah*. This is the first day of the New Year, and a good time for people to look back on the past year and think of all their wrongdoing. By the time of Yom Kippur ten days later Jews should feel that they have put right all their wrongs and that they can stand close to God and confess their sins. Fasting is seen as an aid to worship as it helps take away the need to spend time preparing and eating food. The day of Yom Kippur is so special that every minute should be spent in prayer.

Other religions give up certain foods for a special reason. Lent is a time when many Christians give up rich foods to remember the time when Jesus fasted in

Samina, a Muslim girl, aged 9:
'This is the party we had for Id-ul-fitr. It is a big celebration at the end of Ramadan. During Ramadan we are not supposed to eat anything during the day. I had one meal a day, because I'm only nine, and my little sister ate normally, except she didn't have any sweets or biscuits. At the party we ate the sweets we couldn't have during Ramadan.'

the wilderness. **Orthodox Christians** may give up all meat and animal products at this time. This helps them to think about the time that Jesus was tempted in the wilderness, and his sacrifice of dying for them on the cross.

Hindus can choose whether to take part in fasts. Many fast before a festival, and break their fast by eating the special food that has been offered to the gods for that festival. In some cases, particular foods will be avoided, such as cereals, meat and eggs. By giving up such ordinary foods Hindus feel they are keeping pure, and the festival foods are made special.

*Below* Many Buddhists carry out good deeds by offering food to the monks.

# Glossary

**Ancestors**   People far back in a family's history.

**Blessings**   Special words which are said to make something holy.

**Castes**   Social groups into which Hindu society is divided.

**Communal**   When people do things together.

**Diwali**   The Hindu Festival of Lights.

**Eucharist**   A Christian thanksgiving meal, when they remember Jesus's Last Supper.

**Exodus**   The Jews' escape from slavery in Egypt.

**Five pillars of Islam**   The five most important practices for Muslims.

**Grace**   Words that Christians say before a meal to thank God for the food.

**Gurdwara**   A Sikh temple.

**Gurus**   Hindu or Sikh religious teachers or leaders.

**Halal**   Food that is prepared according to Islamic law.

**Haram**   Food that is not permitted according to Islamic law.

**Incense**   A spice that is burnt to produce a sweet smell.

**Kosher**   Food that is 'clean' according to Jewish law.

**Manger**   A box from which animals feed.

**Orthodox Christians**   Members of the Christian Church based mainly in Eastern Europe.

**Orthodox Jews**   Jews who strictly follow the teachings God revealed to the prophet, Moses.

*Prashad*   Food which has been blessed for Hindus.

**Purified**   Made very clean.

**Resurrection**   The Christian belief that Jesus came back to life after his death.

**Sacrifice**   To give up something important for religious reasons.

**Slaughter**   The killing of animals, especially for food.

**Symbolizes**   Represents or stands for something else.

**Vegetarians**   People who do not eat meat.

**Wilderness**   A wild region where no one lives.

# Further information

## Books to read

The following books will help you find out more about food and fasting:
*Feasting and Fasting* by Jon Mayled (Wayland, 1986)
*Growing up in Islam* by J Ardavan (Longman, 1990)
*Ramadan and Eid ul-Fitr* by Rosalind Kerven (Macmillan Educational, 1986)
*Religious Food* by Jon Mayled and Aviva Paraiso (Wayland, 1987)

These series also contain useful information about the religions dealt with in this book:
*My Belief* (Franklin Watts, 1989)
*Our Culture* (Franklin Watts, 1989)
*Religions of the World* (Simon & Schuster, 1992)

Picture acknowledgements

The publishers wish to thank the following for supplying the photographs in this book:
J Allan Cash 7, 8; John Chorley/University of Wolverhampton 5, 13, 15 top, 17, 22, 26; Eye Ubiquitous 10 (Paul Seheult), 28 (Peter Sanders), 29 (Paul Thompson); Format Partners Photo Library 15 bottom (Maggie Murrary), 16 (Judy Harrison); Hutchison Library 12, 21 top (Liba Taylor), 24 both (top, Liba Taylor); Life File 6 (M Maidment), 9 (Nicola Sutton); Christine Osborne Pictures 18, 19, 20, 27; The Regional R.E. Centre (Westhill College) & Stanley Thornes 23; Skjold Pictures 14; Wayland Picture Library 11 (Jimmy Holmes), 21 bottom (A Hasson), 25 (Julia Waterlow).

# Index

Numbers in **bold** indicate photographs